Circuit Challe

Contents

What is a circuit?

A circuit is a complete loop of wires and different parts. The different parts can include:

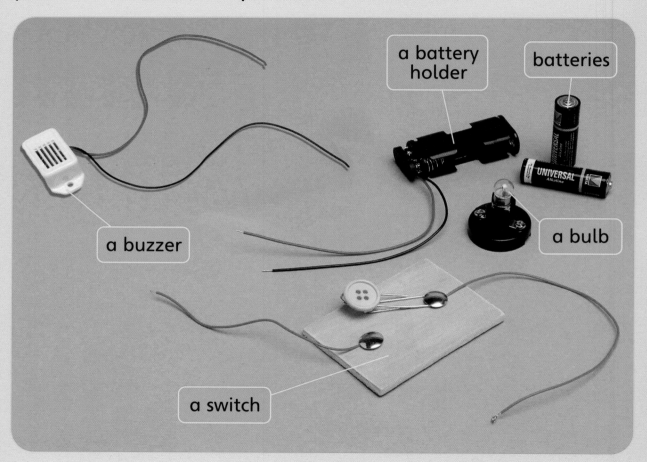

a battery holder

batteries

a buzzer

a bulb

a switch

How does a circuit work?

In a circuit the wires carry electricity from the batteries through the bulb. The bulb lights up because the circuit is complete.

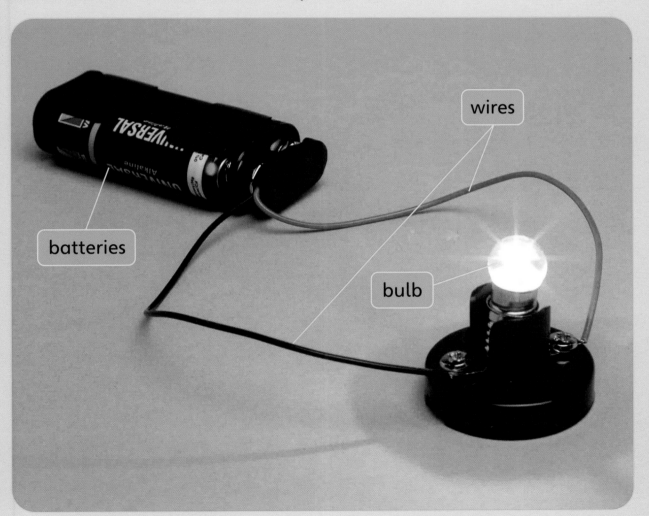

wires

batteries

bulb

How do you connect wires?

To make a circuit you must connect wires. Here are some different methods you can use.

1 Use wires with crocodile clips at the end. Attach the crocodile clips to each screw.

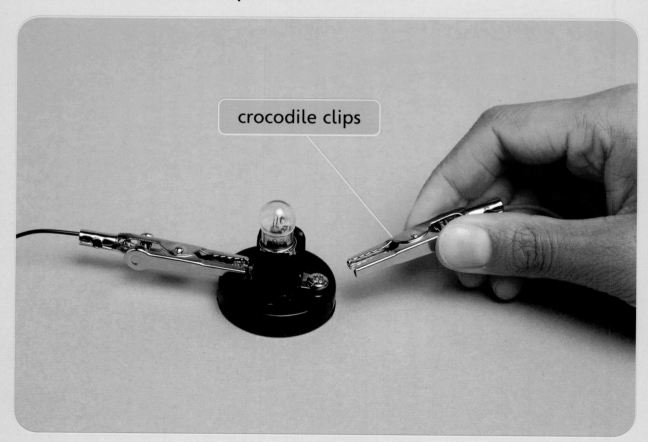

crocodile clips

2 Twist the bare ends of the wires together.

twist

3 Twist the bare ends of the wires around each screw. Tighten each screw with a screwdriver.

screw

twist

5

You will need:

 2 batteries, size D

 1 short wire (5cm) and 1 long wire (15cm)

 1 bulb in a holder

 1 A4 sheet of white paper

 sticky tape

 scissors

 screwdriver

You need to:

1 Tape one battery on top of the other. Put the **+** of the bottom battery on the **−** of the top battery.

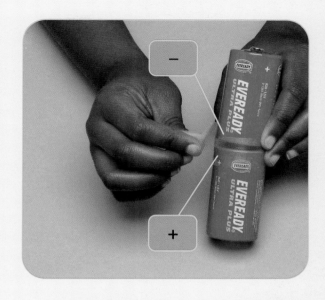

2 Twist the bare end of the long wire around one of the screws of the bulb holder. Tighten the screw with a screwdriver. Connect the short wire to the other screw in the same way.

NEXT

3 Tape the bare end of the short wire to the + on the top battery.

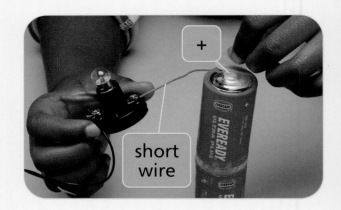

short wire

4 Tape the bulb holder on top of the short wire on the top battery.

5 Cut the paper to the length of the batteries. Wrap the paper round the batteries and the long wire. Fasten with sticky tape.

6 Use your finger to hold the bare end of the long wire onto the ▬ of the bottom battery. Your candle should light up.

7 Pull the wire away to turn the candle off.

OFF

ON

long wire

STOP

You will need:

 2 AA batteries in a battery holder with wires

 1 buzzer with wires

 2 drawing pins

 1 plastic button

 1 large paperclip

 1 wood block (8cm long and 6cm wide)

 sticky tape

You need to:

1 Twist the bare end of one of the wires from the battery holder around the first drawing pin.

2 Push the drawing pin into the wood block.

NEXT

3 Twist the bare end of one of the wires from the buzzer around one end of the paperclip.

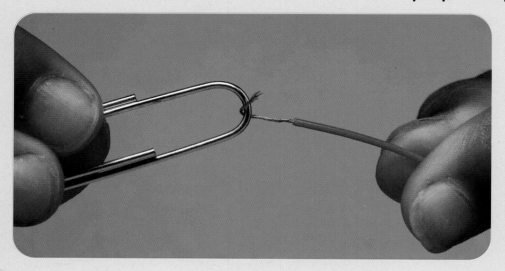

4 Fix the paperclip to the wood block with the second drawing pin.

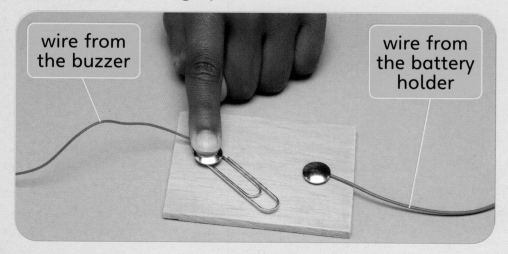

wire from the buzzer

wire from the battery holder

5 Bend the paper clip up so that it does not touch the first drawing pin.

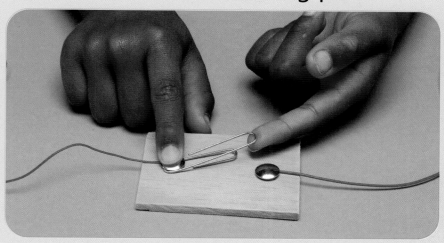

6 Tape a button onto the end of the paper clip. This will be your switch.

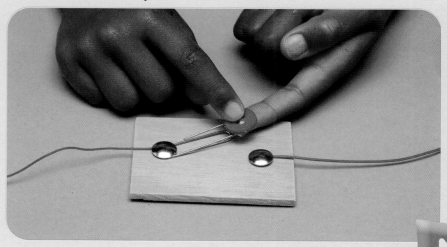

NEXT

7 Connect the wire from the buzzer to the wire from the battery holder. Twist the bare ends of the wires together.

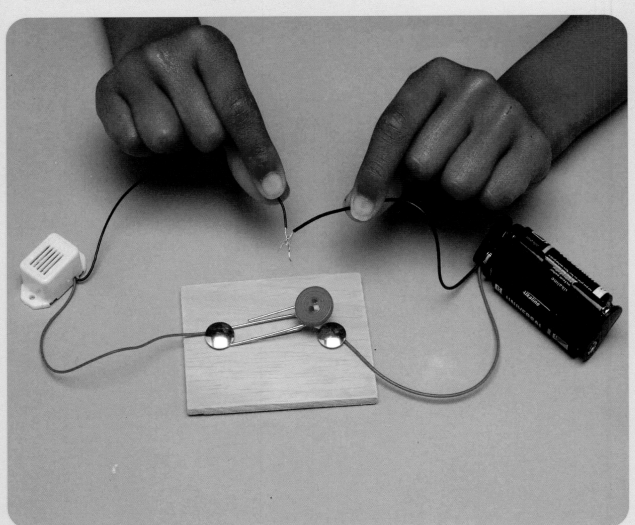

8 Push the button to press the paperclip onto the first drawing pin. Your buzzer should sound.

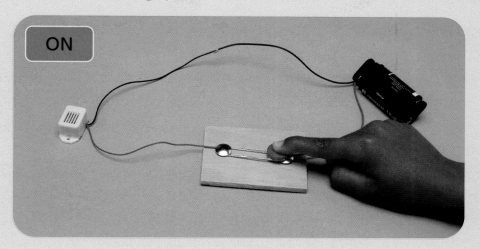

ON

9 Stop pushing the button to turn the buzzer off.

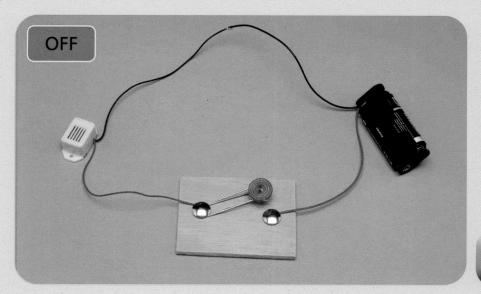

OFF

STOP

Make an electric robot dog

16

You will need:

STEP 1

 glue

 empty boxes and pots

 straw

 scissors

 paint and paint brushes

STEP 2

 1 switch

 2 batteries in a battery holder

 1 long wire

 sticky tape

 2 bulbs in bulb holders

STEP 3

 1 switch

 2 batteries in a battery holder

 1 buzzer with wires

 sticky tape

You need to:

1 Glue some boxes and pots together to make the dog's body, head, nose, ears and legs.

2 Cut out holes for the eyes and tail.

3 Paint the boxes and pots.

NEXT

You need to:

1 To make the dog's eyes, connect:
   (a) the switch to the first bulb holder
   (b) the first bulb holder to the second
       bulb holder
   (c) the second bulb holder to the battery holder
   (d) the battery holder to the switch.

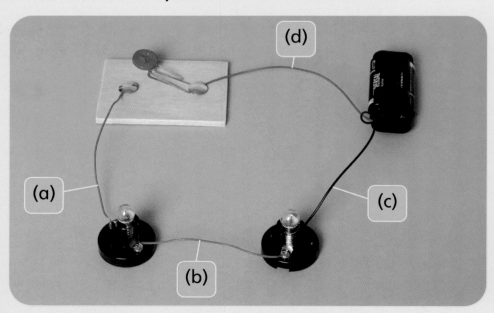

2 Push the bulbs through the dog's eye-holes.

3 Tape the switch onto the side of the dog.

4 Push the button. Your dog's eyes should light up!

NEXT

You need to:

1 To make the dog growl, connect:
   (a) the switch to the battery holder
   (b) the battery holder to the buzzer
   (c) the buzzer to the switch.

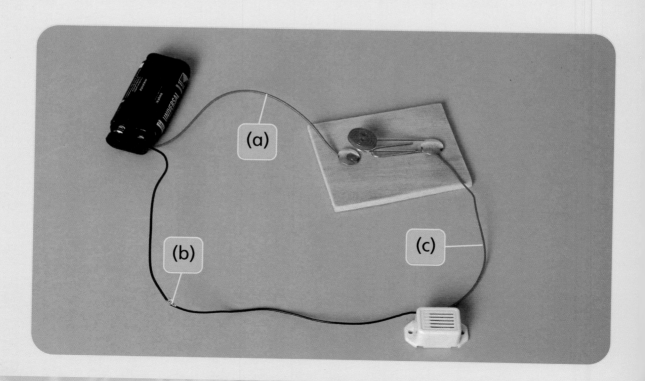

2 Fit the buzzer inside the body of your dog.

3 Tape the switch onto the side of the dog.

4 Push the button. Your dog should growl!

STOP

Index